Am I A Dead Dog?

Jimmy Darnell

RHM

Dedicated To.....

My three special children:

Teresa, with her warm gift of hospitality and entertaining.

Terry, with his deliberate and dedicated drive to study, whether books or the Bible.

Tim, with his passionate pursuit and preaching of Jesus the King.

Contents

Preface – Page 7

The Battle of Jezreel – Page 11

Fear and Panic - Page19

Lodebar – The Desert – Page 27

Something Missing – Page 33

To The Palace – Blessings and Covenant – Page 39

At The King's Table – Page 47

Sin In The Palace – Page 53

Absalom's Rebellion – Page 59

War In The Wilderness – Page 63

The Return Of The King – Page 67

Gibeonites – Page 73

Conclusion – Page 79

Preface

The tale of Mephibosheth in the Old Testament is an exciting story. Set in the days of King David, it has all the elements of a great novel. War, loss, tragic accident, exile, good fortune, revolution and revenge are all part of this adventure story. Mephibosheth, the crippled son of Prince Jonathan, was in the midst of it all.

But most of all the story of Mephibosheth is an Old Testament type of the gospel. It is the story of how a fallen, undeserving, helpless sinner becomes the object of God's redemptive grace, due to a previous blood covenant!

Mephibosheth lost everything when his father Jonathan fell; just as we lost all when our father Adam, as the federal head, fell. Mephibosheth was a helpless cripple. No work could be performed to gain God's (David) favor. His concept of God (David) was wrong. He thought David (God) was his enemy and he was hiding from God (David).

But God (David) came looking for Mephibosheth, not to harm him but to release the covenant blessing of God into his life. God loves the sinner and seeks the sinner. We were not seeking God."... *there is none that seeks after God,"* *Romans 3:11(KJV).* He was, and is, the initiator.

He cut an eternal blood covenant 2000 years ago on a hill called Golgotha. The covenant is between the Father and his eternal son; who became the Son of Man (Jesus) and the representative of fallen man. But the covenant was not only between the Father and Jesus the Son, but with all those in the spiritual loins of Jesus. The covenant is with all those "in Christ". Because of this blood covenant, all the covenant mercies of God – forgiveness, fellowship, healing, deliverance, prosperity, wholeness – flow to us.

But because of our false identity – the dead dog image – it is difficult for us to believe and receive his offer. It's too good to be true. Too often, we continue to live out our false identify rather than believing who we truly are.

This little book will help you move from the false identity of a stinking, worthless, dead dog to your true identity in Christ as a highly favored son or daughter of the king.

What an exciting, life-changing discovery!

Chapter 1

The Battle of Jezreel

"**Y**ou seem nervous, Prince Jonathan", says Elan his armor bearer. "You've sharpened that sword five times now."

"I am a bit nervous. This is a huge Philistine army that has invaded the land. But other than that, several other things have me concerned. Is my covenant friend, David, among the Philistine soldiers? Since he deserted Israel and moved to Gath in the land of the Philistines he has found favor with the Philistine general, Achish. That Philistine knows that David is a mighty warrior who would love to get revenge against my father, Saul. I couldn't blame David after all my father has done against him, but I can't bear the thought of meeting David in battle.

And Dad's mental state is terrible. Ever since he began disobeying the God of Israel his career has gone downhill. Can you imagine how much his jealously of

David has hurt the nation? How much time, energy, manpower and finances has he wasted trying to catch David in the wilderness of Judea? Somehow his expeditions into the desert seeking David always ended up bankrupt. Why would you try to kill your own son-in-law who has been so loyal to our nation? I think the jealousy started when David slew Goliath. David was a great warrior in our army but Dad couldn't handle his success. He heard the women singing the victory song, 'Saul has slain his thousands, but David his ten thousands.'

Now he stays confused and fearful. He's become double-minded – can't make logical decisions. He feels that God has deserted him. He can't get direction from the Lord any more.

Besides all this I'm concerned about my little five year old son, Mephibosheth. If we lose this battle, what will become of him?

I don't know if you heard what happened last night. Saul, the mighty warrior, went to a witch's den at Endor to try and get a word about the battle today. A witch's den! Can you believe that? I don't know what happened last night but I can assure you it wasn't good.

But enough of this talk. The enemy is moving and almost upon us," said Jonathan.

Elam, the armor bearer, pondered all this in his mind. He knew that the real leadership in this massive battle would have to come from Prince Jonathan. After all he was the premier soldier in Israel. None was his equal. He remembered the time when he and Jonathan had attacked a Philistine army all alone. Actually, they had only one sword between them. Saul had a sword but he was wallowing in indecision, so Jonathan decided to attack. When they came over the edge of the canyon, Jonathan drove his sword through the heart of a Philistine soldier.

"I didn't linger. I grabbed the enemy's fallen sword and together we began to hack them to pieces. Wow! What a fight. The enemy army fled and we won the day for Israel," remembered Elam.

"Saul made a stupid vow about no one eating anything until total vengeance was exploited against the enemy. How stupid. Soldiers need energy and we get energy from the food in our pack. Jonathan came upon a bee's nest and ate some honey. His strength really increased. Later his father was going to put him to death for breaking the vow. But all the soldiers and people rescued him. They knew who the real hero was. All that illustrates just what Jonathan was speaking to me about. Saul is confused."

The battle was about to be engaged. Enemy war trumpets were sounding. The clang of shields and swords was distinct. Enemy arrows began to rain from the sky like hailstones in a thunderstorm.

"Elan, come quickly, the enemy is near. I have put Abinadad, my brother, in charge of the east flank. His brave brother, Malchishua, will hold the right flank. We will lead our regiment into the enemy's center with King Saul."

And into the Valley of Jezreel, the ancient Megiddo plain, marched the enemies of the God and nation of Israel. Towering above the valley was Mount Gilboa. The plain of Jezreel, or Megiddo, stretches all the way from the Mediterranean to the Jordan. Many of Israel's battles were fought here. The great final battle between good and evil, Armageddon, will take place here.

At first the Israelites held their ground. Many fought valiantly. But the massive Philistine numbers began to take their toll. Dead and dying soldiers were all around brave Prince Jonathan. They began to fall back onto the mountain. It was their only hope.

"Elan, my son, play the man. Be brave," shouted Jonathan.

"Abinadab, they're breaking through on the left flank. Can you hold?" asked Jonathan. No answer. Jonathan's brave brother was dead.

"Malechishua, the right flank is collapsing. Have you any reinforcements?" shouted Jonathan. Again no answer. The great warrior Malechishua lay dead.

The end came swiftly. King Saul was mortally wounded. Elan was dying. Jonathan tried to run to his Dad's rescue but an enemy arrow found lodging between his shoulders- right into the spine. Jonathan was still alive but paralyzed when a Philistine drove his sword into the heart of the greatest warrior in all of Israel.

It was now all but over. Leaderless, the remnant of Israel's army fled from the battle field. Years before the leader of the nation, King Saul, had forfeited his anointing. Without the anointing the enemies of God prevailed over Israel easily. That leadership anointing rested now on David.

As the scripture says, *"The shield of Saul was not anointed with oil."* (II Samuel 1:21)

WHAT DOES THIS MEAN TO ME?

The anointing of the Holy Spirit is the most precious thing that we possess. There is no substitute for God's powerful presence. It is by the anointing that we can do mighty things. It's by the anointing that we do the works of the kingdom. It's by the anointing that miracles happen. After David's sin with Bathsheba he cried, *"Cast me not away from your presence, and take not your*

Holy Spirit from me." Psalms 51:11 (RSV). He knew that without the anointing he was helpless.

Love the anointing. Cherish it. Don't forfeit it like King Saul did with foolish choices. Continued disobedience, like in Saul's life, will drain the anointing from our lives.

Also, we must learn to follow the cloud of the anointing when it moves. Jonathan knew that the blessing and anointing was no longer on his father's reign. The leadership anointing was now on David. The future was there and Jonathan knew it, but he chose to stay with the old order. And it cost him his life.

Let's be sensitive to the Holy Spirit and move when God moves. To stay with tradition, old forms, family and friends because it is familiar, rather than to move with God, will result in death.

Then Samuel took the horn of oil, and anointed him in the midst of his brothers; and the Spirit of the Lord came mightily upon David from that day forward. I Samuel 16:13 (RSV)

Chapter 2

Fear and Panic

"**I** miss not having a mother," mused Mephibosheth. "I don't even remember her since she died giving birth to me. Some of the kids in the palace can be a little cruel. They snicker about my mother. I miss not having a mother but I do have an awesome dad. He's the crown prince of Israel. Those kids had better not let Dad hear them teasing me. People speak of my dad, Prince Jonathan, with reverence. He's very kind but also a fearsome warrior. Since I'm only five years old I don't know much about his military life. I just know him as Daddy.

Being the son of the crown prince of Israel lets you know that I lack for nothing, except for a mother. Dad sees to it that I have the best of nannies, food and toys. I do have some playmates in the palace. Only a few ever tease me. Michael is my buddy. We love to play war with our wooden swords. My Dad loves to watch us. He likes the thought of me growing up to be a mighty warrior. I hope that happens because I want to please my dad.

Dad's not home right now. He's gone off to war with my grandfather, Saul, and my two uncles, Abinadab and Malchishua. I don't know for sure who the enemy is. Maybe those bad guys called Philistines? But Dad, Grandfather and my two uncles will all be back soon. They always come back.

Even as a five-year-old I can sense that something is wrong. My nanny is upset. She's afraid. Normally, she's so sweet and nice. But now she is on edge. So nervous," thought Mephibosheth.

"Grab some of your toys, Mephibosheth," she yelled. "We're leaving."

"Leaving? Where are we going?" I questioned.

"Don't ask questions," she snapped. "We must go quickly."

"I didn't know that the Philistines had defeated the armies of Israel. I didn't know that Dad, Grandfather and my two uncles were dead.

But my nanny knew. Thinking that the Philistines would soon be at the palace, or more likely thinking that David would arrive to kill all of Saul's family to establish his kingdom, she panicked.

I was not moving fast enough. She scooped me up and began to run. She tripped and I fell to the floor. Oh, what pain! Then I felt nothing. I couldn't feel or move my legs. But I would soon be better, I hoped. But it was not to be; I had received a spinal injury. I would be a cripple all my life."

WHAT DOES THIS MEAN TO ME?

Mephibosheth's nanny allowed fear to grip her. Fear is a real crippler. It is Satan's major weapon against us. Fear will cause us to panic, make poor decisions and do unwise things

Lions roar in the jungle and on the plains of the Serengeti in Africa to strike fear into their prey. Sometimes fear paralyzes the prey, making them easy targets for the devourer. At other times fear causes the little antelopes to panic and run, right into the jaws of other lions waiting in ambush.

Fear is a paralyzing power.

Fear will bind you and keep you from Kingdom victory. Fear will keep you from reaching your goals in life.

Fear of rejection, fear of the dark, fear of water, fear of heights, fear of people, fear of driving, fear of insects, fear of dogs or fear of storms. Fear of anything. Satan uses irrational phobias to bind us.

Early in my ministry I was confronted with the intimidating, paralyzing power of fear. After graduating from Southwestern Baptist Theological Seminary, my wife, Beth, and I moved to Lake Lyndon B. Johnson in the Texas Hill Country to pastor the Buckner Boys Ranch Baptist Church.

The church ministered to the boys who came to live at the ranch, staff and people from the surrounding community. The boys at the ranch were not true orphans; they were broken- home orphans. Over 80 percent came from alcoholic homes. Most of them had deep mental, emotional and spiritual needs.

After I had been pastor for several months, a young man named Bill came to live at the Buckner Ranch. He was junior high age. Bill came from an abusive home situation and was glad to be in a place where he had three square meals, people who loved him and a 4,000-acre ranch to enjoy. He was an obedient boy, and fit into the ranch routine well.

Several months after his arrival, Bill began to have headaches. The headaches soon became more frequent and increasingly severe. Whenever a headache hit him, his body would become totally paralyzed. Eventually, he had a headache almost continually and lay paralyzed in the dorm.

We called in the very best doctors. After multiple tests and examinations, the physical doctors gave their evaluation.

"Bill is a normal, healthy, 14-year old boy. There is nothing physically wrong with him," they said.

Big help! "Nothing physically

wrong." He was just crippled, that's all.

So we called in the psychiatrists. They ran a battery of tests on Bill. After several weeks of testing and counseling, the psychiatrists gave their evaluation.

"Bill is suffering from what we call in our profession 'hysterical conversions'. Bill has a deep rooted fear of his father and when he begins to think about his father, fears well up in him causing his head to hurt and his body to be paralyzed," they explained.

They learned that Bill's father was a very cruel man. He had beaten the boy unmercifully. Several times he had made a whip of barbed wire and whipped Bill. No wonder he was afraid of the man.

Talk about the paralyzing power of fear. We had a perfectly healthy 14-year-old who became totally paralyzed when the fear of his father overwhelmed him.

But the story has a good ending.

We committed Bill to the state mental hospital in Austin, Texas, for 30 days. As his pastor, I drove to Austin to see him on the first day that he could have visitors.

Bill greeted me with a remarkable story.

"That night when you left me here, I was scared to death," he said. "They put me in a ward with people that had severe problems. During the night people were groaning, shrieking and screaming."

Bill continued, "I was so scared that I rolled out of bed, got on my knees and prayed from my heart 'Dear Jesus, I'm so alone and so frightened. Please help me.'"

It was a simple prayer, but Bill said suddenly the ward was filled with light. Bill, the cripple, got up and began to walk. He wasn't crippled anymore. The doctors were amazed. They didn't know what they had done.

We know what happened. Jesus, the Deliverer, responded to the desperate cry of a frightened, 14-year-old boy that night and delivered him from the spirit of fear.

I brought Bill back to the ranch, baptized him, and he became one of the leading young men at the Buckner Boys Ranch during his years there.

Don't submit to fear. *"God has not given us the spirit of fear; but of power, and of love, and of a sound mind."* II Timothy 1:7 (KJV). Fear comes from the devil. Cast it out in Jesus' name.

Renew your thinking with anti-fear Scriptures, like, *"perfect love casts out fear."* I John 4:18. The Bible is full of them.

I sought the Lord and he answered me, and delivered me from all my fears. Psalms 34:4 (RSV)

Chapter 3

Lodebar – The Desert

"**I**t didn't take us long to vacate the palace. We crossed the Jordan River in the darkness and traveled into the wilderness. Where would we go? Then we got a break. A family friend, Machir the son of Ammiel, sent word for us to join him and his family at the desert outpost of Lodebar. It sure wasn't the palace, but in our situation, it was like heaven – at least at first.

In all my years of growing up in Lodebar I was always told that 'David is your enemy. As a descendent of Saul, you are a threat to the Davidic kingdom.' I lived under a shroud of fear of the day that David might discover my hideout.

I'm thankful for faithful family servants who took care of me. But growing up without a mother and, now without a father, has been really tough. I guess I was an orphan.

My feet never got well.   I was permanently paralyzed from my waist down. I never got to play games with the other boys at Lodebar. All I could do was watch.   As I grew older, I couldn't work like the other boys.   It looked like fun feeding and watering the camels, donkeys and other livestock, but I was just a helpless cripple.

As teenagers the other boys would go hunting for gazelles.   I would have loved to hunt. I learned to shoot a bow but never got to go on the hunts into the desert.

One day one of the family servants came running to the tent. 'Quickly, hide Mephibosheth.   David's   soldiers   are passing through the village.'

They were not looking for me but just a glimpse of the royal insignia of the House of David on their shields sent fear through my body. My friends covered me with rugs until all was clear. How many years would I have to live like this? Could you call this living?

I was approaching age 20 when I met   this   really   pretty,   Bedouin   girl, namedCora.   I never had been around many girls, only women caretakers.   My hormones really began to stir when I saw Cora at the water well.   Some of my friends arranged for me to meet her. It didn't take long before we fell in love. She was so kind to me and my handicap didn't seem to bother her.   For the first time in 15 years, I felt some happiness. We married quickly and in less than a year our son Mica was born.   I was so proud of him.

But Cora and I began to have trouble. It wasn't long until it seemed we were fighting all the time.   She tried to keep the home peaceful but my inner struggles of worthlessness just couldn't be overcome.   I could have married anyone and the marriage would have fallen apart. I was a real mess mentally and emotionally.   I felt like I was no good. Eventually, the marriage failed.   But I still have Mica and I love him very much, "said Mephibosheth with genuine gratitude.

WHAT DOES THIS MEAN TO ME?

Mephibosheth   is   not   the   only

person who ever suffered from feelings of inadequacy, insecurity and no self worth. A successful marriage is tough enough even for two well-adjusted, mature people. Marriage is in trouble in America. When people marry who had no positive role model of a father and mother, the marriage starts in the negative. If two young people with negative, failure identities marry- except for a miracle- the marriage will fail. Their insecurities will devour each other.

Lodebar means "without pasture." For people with severe identity problems, their best hope is to leave Lodebar and get in an environment of hope and love. Find rich pastures full of teaching about Jesus and His covenant love. In this surrounding of hope they can be healed and learn how to affirm their children.

It is very important that we affirm our children every day. Discovering our true identity in Christ is vital. Helping young people to embrace a positive, Christ-centered identity will help them live happy, productive lives.

Often life's circumstances, negative parents or teasing and bullying by other children reinforce negative self identity. Help your children see who God says they are. Help them tear down negative identities and become healthy, whole young men and women.

No, in all these things we are more than conquerors through him who loved us. Romans 8:37 (RSV)

Chapter 4

Something Missing

Many years had passed since David became King of Israel, as God had promised. He became very successful and powerful. All of Israel's historic enemies were defeated and subdued. The wealth of the nations flowed now into Israel and King David. Many sons and daughters were his delight. What more could a king ask for?

Then one day David awakened to realize something was missing. And he asked this question – "Is there still anyone left of the house of Saul, that I may show him covenant mercy for Jonathan's sake?"

Many years before, while yet teenagers, David and Jonathan had become best friends. God knit their souls together. They hunted together, feasted together, and went to war together.

But the memory of Jonathan that never faded in David's heart was the day he and Prince Jonathan cut blood covenant. That covenant was ever on David's mind. Although it had been almost 30 years since they cut the covenant, it seemed like yesterday to David.

When they cut the covenant the first thing they did was to exchange robes. Jonathan was the Crown Prince of Israel and when David put on his robe it was as if he robed himself in dignity and royalty.

Then they exchanged weapon belts. As David girded himself with Jonathan's belt, from which hung his sword, dagger and sling, he felt strength and power surge through him. After all, Jonathan was the premier soldier of all Israel.

Then the two friends took a sword and split an animal right down through the head and backbone. Laying the two halves across from each other, they walked into the path of blood, raised their right hands toward heaven, and made a cut on their right wrists. Now standing in blood, with blood running down their forearms, they began to make covenant vows to each other. They vowed ever to be loyal to each other. They vowed ever to support and protect each other. They pledged their lives, fortunes and sacred honor to each other.

After these vows, they called down curses upon each other. "If ever we violate these vows that we have made today, may God Almighty split us in half like this animal we stand between."

Finally, they ate a covenant meal of bread and wine together.

Realizing that he had not cut that covenant only with Jonathan as an individual but also with Jonathan's seed - even though neither was married with children at that time - David asks the question about showing covenant mercy to anyone remaining of the house of Saul. And he asks the question, 'for Jonathan's sake.'

Soon a former servant of the house of Saul, named Ziba, came forward with vital information. "There is still a son of Jonathan; but he is crippled in his feet," said Ziba. David could not contain his excitement and blurted out, "Where is he?"

That's when he learned that this son of Jonathan had been living with Machir, the son of Ammiel, at Lodebar for almost 20 years. Wow! 20 years! All that time Mephibosheth could have been living with King David in the palace.

Soon a royal chariot was on the way to Lodebar to bring Mephibosheth to Jerusalem.

WHAT DOES THIS MEAN TO ME?

Real friendship, like that between David and Jonathan is one of life's treasures. In life we make many acquaintances but real friends are rare. Some are fair weather friends. They are your friends, only as long as the relationship benefits them. But true friendship will even transcend death.

Build good friendships and relationships. A person who has good relationships with parents, friends, co-workers, and authorities will have a good life. But the person whose life is a trail of broken relationships will have a miserable life. That person is always mad at somebody. Blame is projected to others.

It's always someone else's fault.

Remember, he that would have friends must show himself friendly. Be a real friend and the Father will add loyal friends to your life.

Your friend, and your father's friend, do not forsake... *Proverbs 27:10 (RSV)*

Chapter 5

To The Palace

Blessings And Covenant

Panic broke out in the household of Machir, the son of Ammiel, when the chariot from the King's headquarters entered Lodebar. Swiftly, soldiers were at the door.

"We are looking for the man named Mephibosheth?"   they   questioned. Servants began to run. But the one the king was seeking couldn't run. He was a cripple.

"I am Mephibosheth," I answered.

"Your presence is demanded at the palace of King David," they shouted.

"Strong   arms   grabbed   me   and placed me into the chariot. I wasn't permitted to even pack a night bag. Back across the Judean desert sped the chariot as sand flew behind the wheels. Then we forded the Jordan River that I had crossed so many years ago as a five-year-old. Then on to Jerusalem.

Jerusalem was made the capital of Israel by David after he was anointed king. As the chariot rattled down the stone-paved streets my fear and insecurities went ballistic. I was literally shaking. I knew what awaited me. Death was near. The day I had feared all those years had now arrived.

The soldiers carried me into the palace and placed me in a chair facing the most powerful king on earth. I knew the death sentence was coming. Then I heard these words come out of King David's mouth. 'Mephibosheth, don't be afraid. I don't want to harm you; I want to bless you. I am going to show you covenant kindness for the sake of your father Jonathan. Everything that you lost when your grandfather, Saul, and father, Jonathan, died in battle that day, I restore it back to you. All the land that belonged to Saul, the king, is now yours. Mephibosheth, you are now a rich man. And I don't want you living out there in the desert like an outcast. You are to move to Jerusalem and into the palace.

You will live with me. And you will eat at my table always, like one of the sons of the king.'"

"I couldn't believe my ears. My response came right out of my warped identity. 'Why would you show such kindness to a dead dog like me?'" I asked.

"If I had been one of your faithful men, like those who followed you into exile when Saul was trying to kill you all those years, then I would know that you are rewarding me for my love and faithfulness to you. But sir, I have not been one of your faithful servants. The truth is that I have feared and hated you. I have always considered you my enemy. I don't understand why you show me, just a lowly dead dog, such kindness?" I cried.

Then David began to speak. "I will tell you why. Mephibosheth, I know you don't remember much about your dad because you were only five years old when he died. But your father, Jonathan, was my closest friend. He was the Prince of Israel and the mightiest warrior in the land. We loved each other. Then one day we cut blood covenant. As a son of Israel, you know what was involved in that covenant. When we cut our wrists and raised our hands toward heaven, I swore ever to show loyalty and covenant mercy to Jonathan. But when I made those vows, I did not cut covenant with Jonathan only as an individual. I cut covenant with all those potentially in his loins. I cut that covenant with his seed – his descendants.

For many years now I have looked at this covenant scar on my wrist and I have longed to find one of Jonathan's descendants so that I could pour out on him the abundant, covenant kindness of God. And now I have found you."

"It just seemed too good to be true. But it was true. I had a hard time really believing that this miraculous change was due to a blood covenant cut years before I was even conceived. My terrible mental-emotional picture of myself as a no-good, dead dog was like a roadblock to the truth," lamented Mephibosheth.

WHAT DOES THIS MEAN TO ME?

Two thousand years ago, God the Father cut blood covenant with his eternal son, now become the Son of Man (Jesus) and the representative of the fallen race of Adam. The Father did not cut the covenant with us as individuals. If the covenant is between the Father and you and me as individuals we would mess up our part quickly. But the covenant is between the Father and the Son. That's why the book of Hebrews can speak of 'the blood of the everlasting covenant.' The Father will never falter on his end. Jesus will always be faithful to keep his part of the covenant. It will never be broken. That's awesome news; but there is more. Not only did the Father cut blood covenant with his son, who is our representative, but he cut covenant with all those in the spiritual loins of Jesus. He cut covenant with all who are "in Christ". All the covenant mercies of God flow to us who are in Christ. Forgiveness of sin, deliverance from oppression, freedom from poverty, healing from diseases, and a new identity as highly favored sons and daughters of the King, are all provided by the covenant of being "in Christ". What good news!

It almost sounds too good to be true. Our response is often like

Mephibosheth. "How could all this be for a dead dog like me?"

The dead dog image was a lie. The truth was that Mephibosheth was the grandson of a king, the son of the crown prince of Israel, and a highly- favored friend of King David. That was the truth.

But the old dead dog identity tries to hang on to us. Think about a dead dog on the side of the highway. It's never a pretty sight. It is bloated, covered with blood and flies, tongue hanging out, intestines strewn across the road. How awful! But the devil and circumstances always try to program this false identity into us. But our true DNA is covenant. We are loved, accepted and blessed in Christ.

Believe who you really are, and you will become who you really are.

I have a Labrador retriever named Annie. I bought Annie when she was only five months old. Her registration papers showed that she had the DNA of a champion. Both parents had earned Master Hunter certificates. She came from National Champion kennels in both mother and father lineage.

Annie had the most intelligence, energy, speed and desire to hunt of any dog that I had ever trained. But her behavior did not match her DNA. She did not act like who she really was. She was wild. Training her was very difficult. Her first two years of duck hunting were not good. But as I worked and walked with her each day I spoke over her that she had the DNA of a champion. "You will be the best duck retriever that I have ever trained," I would say.

With discipline and love I continued to work with Annie. I wouldn't give up, even when her behavior was bad, because I knew what was in her. When she chewed up the neighbor's water hose, ran away, played keep-away with fallen birds, and barked in the blind, I would not give up.

God never gives up on us because he knows what he has put in us – his Spirit, his DNA.

Now Annie is five years old and she has become a champion. Her behavior is matching her DNA. She has become who she really is.

Believe your new identity in Christ. You are not a stinking failure; a dead dog. You are a highly- favored son of the King. Believe it. Say it. And you will become who you really are.

Also remember, even though Mephibosheth thought David was his enemy, David went seeking this helpless one. Covenant is like that. God comes looking for the sinner. He pursues us, even when we think we are dead dogs. His love knows no boundaries.

Therefore if any man be in Christ, he is a new creation; old things are passed away; behold, all things are become new. II Corinthians 5:17 (KJV)

Chapter 6

At The King's Table

"**K**ing David quickly sent a wagon to Lodebar to bring my few possessions and my son, Mica. It was great when Mica joined me in the palace. I told him about my good fortune. He couldn't believe it either.

That first night in our own spacious rooms, with luxurious beds, was so awesome. But the thought kept hiding in the corner of my brain, 'What is a dead dog like me doing in a place like this?'

But things began to change slowly in my heart as Mica and I sat each day at the king's table. I came to know King David as a good and kind man. We began to grow closer as time passed. I no longer feared him. I knew he truly wanted the best for me. After meals, the king and I often lingered and had sweet fellowship. I missed him when he would go off to war for weeks at a time.

Life is good here with David in the palace. I have a servant named Ziba, who was a servant in my grandfather's administration. David put him over my whole estate. I don't have to worry about the property or the crops. Ziba takes care of all that. It has made me a rich man. I'm living a dream. This new environment of hope has become a tree of life for me. I'm now in a real family.

I love my association with David's sons. They have come to accept me like I was their brother. I'm older than them but being around these teenagers makes me feel young. I am especially close to Chileab. His mother is Abigail, the widow of Nabal of Carmel. I think she is the most beautiful of all David's wives. I know the story of how David met her when he lived in the wilderness fleeing from my grandfather.

She was married to a harsh and surly man named Nabal. Nabal treated David and all his men with cruelty and disrespect. David was about to kill him when Abigail placed herself between David and Nabal. She assured David that he would someday be king and persuaded him not to shed Nabal's blood. David heeded her intercession. Soon Nabal died of a stroke and David married beautiful Abigail.

David's oldest son, Amnon, I keep at a distance. I don't trust him. There is something in him that is wicked. I don't know what it is, but I don't like it. Time will reveal if I'm right.

Absalom, David's third son, is the most handsome, brave and adventurous of all the boys. He is highly intelligent and has a commanding presence. He lights up the room when he walks in. He is also very ambitious. But he is the king's favorite. Whatever Absalom wants, his father gives.

Because of my linage in Saul's house he seems suspicious of me .Maybe not. But I can't seem to shake that thought.

Adonijah, David's fourth son, and I get along okay. But he seems to carry a chip on his shoulder. I think he resents Absalom being the king's favorite.

Chileab even took me gazelle hunting. He lifted me into his chariot and we chased the swift gazelles. I finally got off a good shot. The arrow sunk into the antelope's heart. I was so proud. We ate the gazelle that night at the king's table. Everyone was proud of me.

The years began to slip by quickly. Then tragedy struck the palace."

WHAT DOES THIS MEAN TO ME?

The primary benefit of our covenant salvation is fellowship with our king. Above all else, he is our treasure. He wants us to dine with him at his table with other daughters and sons in his family.

Jesus said, *"Behold I stand at the door and knock; if anyone hears my voice and opens the door, I will come in to him and eat with him, and he with me. Revelation 3:20 (RSV)*

The Greek word used for eat or sup (KJV) is for the evening meal. In the Greco- Roman world breakfast was brief, the mid-day meal was usually eaten hurriedly on the street but the supper meal was the meal where there was time to visit, talk and fellowship. It is to this fellowship meal to which Jesus invites us.

The evangelist, Mark, records that Jesus appointed the twelve to be with him and to be sent out to preach and have authority to cast out demons. (3:14-15) Notice that first of all they were called to be with him – fellowship. Out of this relationship ministry would follow.

Prayer is not a shopping list of needs presented to the Almighty. Yes, he wants us to bring our requests with thanksgiving. But most of all he just wants to be with us. Enjoy his presence at the table.

Also remember that Mephibosheth's crippled feet were not visible when they were under the King's table. All our weaknesses, infirmities and insecurities fade out of sight when we fellowship with Him at his table.

The table is prepared. The banquet is spread. The king is present. Come now to the table.

He brought me to the banqueting house, and his banner over me was love. Song of Solomon 2:4 (RSV)

Chapter 7

Sin In The Palace

It all started in a time of idleness. Instead of leading the armies of Israel into battle as he always did, King David sent General Joab and the army to attack the Ammonite city of Rabbah. He stayed in Jerusalem at the palace. Mephibosheth later heard what happened.

David was on the rooftop terrace when he saw a beautiful woman named Bathsheba, bathing. She lived in a house a few doors down from the palace. David brought her to the palace and one thing led to another. Soon they were in bed together. A few weeks later Bathsheba's servant brought word to the king that Bathsheba was pregnant. David quickly came up with a plan to pin the pregnancy on her husband, Uriah the Hittite. Uriah was one of David's mighty men and a good friend of the king. David sent word to Joab to send Uriah home on leave. Just for a little rest and relaxation. But instead of Uriah going home and sleeping with his beautiful wife, he slept in the servant quarters of the palace. David got word that he didn't go home.

"Have you not come from a long journey? Why did you not go down to your house?" asked David.

Uriah replied, that while the ark of God, and Joab and the army were camping in the open field, how could he go home to eat, drink and sleep with his wife?

Mephibosheth didn't know if he was really such a great patriot or if he was suspicious, but he would not go home. So that night David invited him to a banquet, got him drunk, thinking that now he will stagger home. Not so. He stayed with the palace servants again.

Then David did something that Mephibosheth thought would not be possible of his king. He sent Uriah back to the battlefield with a letter to General Joab, telling Joab to put Uriah in harm's way and then pull all support troops back. Now alone, Uriah died at the hand of the enemy.

Immorality and murder - at least that's the way Mephibosheth heard the story. It was hard for him to believe.

WHAT DOES THIS MEAN TO ME?

Sin is so deceptive. Sin will always take us farther than we planned to go. I do not think David planned to sleep with Bathsheba at first. He simply inquired about the woman. Immediately God gave him a warning. A servant replied, "Is not this Bathsheba, the wife of Uriah the Hittite?" God was saying, "Leave her alone. This is your good friend's wife."

Then he invited her to the palace, probably only to visit with her. Like a simple lunch with a female co-worker. But one thing led to another –then adultery.

Sin will always keep us longer than we planned to stay. David probably thought, "Well, that's over now. Just a brief moral failure, no more to be spoken of. It was just a simple one-night stand."

Not so. Soon the message – "I am pregnant". Oh my, this thing is not going away. David developed intricate plans to trap Uriah and blame the pregnancy on him. But nothing worked. Panic. Now it's on to murder. He had not planned on any of this.

Also, sin will cost you more than you can afford to pay. Though forgiven of his sin, terrible consequences continued. Death of the child from the adulterous relationship, rape of the king's daughter, Tamar, by her half-brother, Amnon, murder of Amnon by Tamar's brother, Absalom, banishment of Absalom from the kingdom and Absalom's rebellion and death. As David cried "O Absalom. O Absalom my son. Would that I had died instead of you". He is saying, "My sin is costing me more than I can afford to pay."

When confronted with his sin by the prophet Nathan, David did repent. His fellowship with the God of Israel was restored but the consequences of his sin were far reaching. It set things in motion that had terrible repercussions on the king's family. But, by far, the worst, consequence of the sin was Absalom's loss of respect for his father. That seed of rebellion was planted in that proud teenage boy by his father's sin. Many brave soldiers would also die because of this.

Our example before our children is so important. Consistency of character is pre-eminent. Moral failure can cause our children and friends to lose respect for us. But even at our worst, our God is still faithful. His love and forgiveness knows no boundaries. *"Where sin abounds, grace does much more abound." Romans 5:20* (KJV). Our repentance looses a flood of forgiveness, grace and restoration. Our joy is restored. Fellowship with the king is restored. We are now able to sing with David the psalmist, *"Blessed is the man whose transgression is forgiven, whose sin is covered." Psalms 32:1(RSV)*

"He removes our sins as far as the east is from the west." Psalms 103:12 If the Bible had said, "he removes our sins as far as the north is from the south," then the distance could be measured in miles from North Pole to South Pole. But there is no east pole or west pole. So the distance is infinite.

But we must always remember that the consequences of sin often continue, even after we are forgiven. So let's stay close to the king.   Avoid sin.   Live righteous.

Fathers, do not provoke your children to anger, but bring then up in the discipline and instruction of the Lord. Ephesians 6:4 (RSV)

Chapter 8

Absalom's Rebellion

David loved Absalom above all his other children. Eventually, he allowed Absalom to return back to Jerusalem after the murder of his brother, Amnon. But he didn't discern what was in Absalom's heart.

Absalom began a calculated plan to steal the Kingdom from his father. Every day he would position himself at the gate of the Holy City and intercept the people as they came from various regions and provinces to talk to King David about their problems. Being very persuasive, he would say something like this: "You do have a valid complaint. You have suffered much injustice. But my Dad is just too busy to care for the people any more. But if I were king, I would see that you receive justice in your case."

And he would entice them and kiss them. Thus, he stole the hearts of the men of Israel from his father. It was disloyalty of the highest order.

The day came when the rebel prince sounded the trumpets in Israel calling for revolution. He raised a huge rebel army and marched on the city of Jerusalem.

It totally caught King David off guard. A wild scramble of residents began to evacuate Jerusalem. David and a band of loyal friends fled from the Holy City and across the Jordan into the wilderness, as Absalom was entering Jerusalem.

"I told my servant, Ziba, to saddle a mule for me to flee with the king. But Ziba deceived me. He went with David and left me in the palace. What a distressing hour. My Lord the king is gone and now I will have to face Absalom alone. He knows I am the legitimate heir to the throne of Saul. I am a threat to his selfish plans. Will he kill me? I must hide quickly," lamented Mephibosheth.

WHAT DOES THIS MEAN TO ME?

Disloyalty is a terrible sin. It usually spurns goodness and kindness shown to one. It is often on the sly; it's a stab in the back.

To abandon a friend is disloyalty. To speak evil of a friend is disloyalty or to violate the trust of a friend is disloyalty.

In betraying Jesus to the Jewish authorities, Judas displayed gross disloyalty. Jesus loved Judas. He saw in him the potential of a great apostle. But Judas became disappointed with Jesus because of his continued emphasis on a spiritual Kingdom. "Let's see some action. Let's move against the Romans in revolution," thought Judas. But Jesus never met those expectations. So Judas, seeking to salvage something after following a visionary fool for three whole years, betrayed Jesus for 30 pieces of silver.

When an associate pastor, who has been given a place in ministry by the senior pastor, splits off part of the membership and starts a new church, he is guilty of disloyalty and betrayal. God is not pleased with such. It is the spirit of Absalom.

When a man abandons the wife of his youth for another woman, he is guilty of disloyalty. Marriage involves a covenant. To violate that covenant is a disloyal act.

Let's be loyal, covenant-keeping people. That's how our God is.

But It'tai answered the king. "As the Lord lives, and as my lord the king lives, wherever my lord the king shall be, whether for death or for life, there also will your servant be." II Samuel 15:21 (RSV)

Chapter 9

War In The Wilderness

"**A**bsalom entered Jerusalem like a conquering king. Some of David's friends supported him. Ahithophel, Bathsheba's grandfather and David's trusted counselor, switched his support to Absalom. The rebellion grew in size and intensity. I hid out in a cellar of the palace. Maybe Absalom would not find me," recounted Mephibosheth.

"I knew a great battle was going to be fought in the wilderness between the loyal forces of King David and the rebel army of Absalom. David had with him some powerful generals and mighty warriors. Absalom may have had the upper hand but all was not lost for the king."

As David prepared his army for battle, the king's last words of instruction to his commanders were "Deal gently for my sake with Absalom. I know he's a rebel. I know he deserves to die. But he's still my son."

Two great armies clashed on the field of battle that day. It was a bloody day but the rebel forces of Absalom were defeated by David's army. Absalom sought to escape. He was riding his mule through a thick oak forest when his long, flowing hair tangled in the branches and his mule rode out from under him. Absalom was left hanging, suspended between heaven and earth. That hair, that he had been so proud of, became his downfall.

One of David's soldiers discovered him but dared not lift his hand against the rebel. He had heard the king's final instructions. But he went and told Joab, who was a blood- thirsty, military genius. The soldier took Joab to the suspended Absalom and Joab threw three darts into Absalom's heart. David's son died that day.

When David heard the news of the victory he was elated. But when he heard that Absalom was dead he began to weep and moan. "O my son Absalom, my son, my son Absalom! Would I had died instead of you, O Absalom, my son, my son?"

WHAT DOES THIS MEAN TO ME?

David spoiled Absalom, his favorite son. He never corrected him. Absalom's vanity and pride were allowed to run unbridled.

We all make mistakes with our children. But regardless of their character defects, rebellion, ungratefulness and sin, we still love them. Which of us in David's situation would not have instructed the army – "Deal gently with the young man Absalom?" And who among us in deep grief would not have cried out "O Absalom, O Absalom my son. I would rather have died instead of you?"

David's love for Absalom is like the Father's love for us, his children. He wants the best for us. He yearns over us.

Let's love our children, discipline our children, suffer long with our children, forgive our children, and pray that they not meet the tragic end of Absalom.

A righteous man who walks in his

integrity- blessed are his sons after him!
Proverbs 20:7 (RSV)

Chapter 10

The Return Of The King

All of Jerusalem waited eagerly for news concerning the battle. Would Absalom be king now? Or did King David prevail? Soon messengers arrived announcing that Absalom was dead. David and his loyal band were on the way to Jerusalem.

"Now out of my hiding closet, I determined to be the first person to greet the king. I knew he would be grieving over Absalom. Maybe I could encourage him. But I looked like a mess. I was in such distress over the whole Absalom rebellion that I had not even changed my clothes, trimmed my beard or dressed my crippled feet.

I was finally able to get someone to saddle a mule for me and I met the king just as the great hordes of warriors were crossing the Jordan. They all looked weary but triumphant at the same time. Ittai, the Gittite, a foreigner who had become a loyal friend to Kind David, rode beside the king. I met him once at the palace and was so impressed with his devotion to the king and the God of Israel.

David's other two generals, Joab and Abishai, his brother, also followed near the king. Joab I fear, but Abishai I respect. He's a tough, brave, straight-forward fighter who several times had put his life on the line for the king.

David immediately asked me the question that I knew he would," reasoned Mephibosheth.

"Why did you not go with me, Mephibosheth?"

"It was a legitimate question. After all, for years I had set at the king's table with his sons. It was all because of his covenant mercy that I was even alive," assessed Mephibosheth.

"I wanted to ride with you but my servant, Ziba, deceived me. Knowing I was crippled he just left me to die at the hand of Absalom," I replied.

Ziba had slandered Mephibosheth

to the king. He lied and told David that he tried to get Mephibosheth to come but Mephibosheth said that he was staying to regain the kingdom of Israel that was rightly his. What a lie! Absalom was not about to let a crippled son of Jonathan become king. Mephibosheth would not even have a plea. Death was certain had Absalom found him.

"Obviously, either Ziba or I was lying. David, although usually very perceptive, couldn't discern who was telling the truth. So he divided the property between us. Ziba was now rich due to his lying tongue. He's no longer my servant. But I still have plenty to support Mica and me. Continuing to have wealth was not my greatest joy. Ziba could have it all. I was just happy that the king had come safely home.

For the next several years it seemed like that my relationship with David was a little strained. Did David have a disloyal man sitting at his table? I'm sure those thoughts passed through his mind, but he continued to show covenant kindness to me.

One fall morning David's son,

Chileab, and I were in his chariot hunting gazelles. A band of Bedouins approached our chariot. To my surprise and delight I saw a beautiful woman in the band. It was Cora. We had a wonderful reunion. I told her about all the wonderful things that had happened in my life due to David's blood covenant with my dad, Jonathan," recounted Mephibosheth.

"I am a different man than the one you married years ago," I said. "I'm healed, whole and happy on the inside."

Life had not been easy for Cora. She had a brief relationship with a prosperous Bedouin. She thought he was a good man but he turned out to be evil. Her hopes were dashed again. But through it all, she remained the same sweet Cora.

"You can guess what happened. We fell in love again. Soon we were remarried and she joined Mica and me in the palace. Kind David was happy to receive her. She was now older, more mature, but still beautiful. I am a blessed man.

Mica did not recall anything about

his mother, because he was so young when Cora and I parted ways. But she was delighted to be mother again to her son, even though he was now older. They are so happy together."

WHAT DOES THIS MEAN TO ME?

David could have easily dismissed Mephibosheth from his presence and the palace. But he didn't. The covenant made with Jonathan and his seed was more powerful than any suspected disloyalty on the part of Mephibosheth.

Even in times of tension, and perhaps failure on our part, the everlasting covenant guarantees our security. We are not kicked out of the family. The table of fellowship still beckons us. Our God is "... *long-suffering, not willing that any should perish."* II Peter 3:9 (KJV)

I will sing of the steadfast love (Hebrew checed i.e. covenant) of the Lord forever; with my mouth I will proclaim your faithfulness to all generations. For your steadfast love (covenant love) was established forever, your faithfulness is firm as the heavens. Psalms 89:1-2 (RSV)

Chapter 11

Gibeonites

Many years after Absalom's rebellion, famine gripped the land of Israel for three years. David's reign had always been blessed with prosperity and plenty. And now famine stalked the land. Why? That's the question that King David asked the Lord. Israel was a covenant people and their land was covenant land. How can there be famine in a covenant land?

God gave David the answer. "There is bloodguilt on Saul and his house because he put the Gibeonites to death."

To understand this we have to go far back in Israel's history: Joshua and the armies of Israel crossed the Jordan River into the Promise Land with a mandate from God Almighty. "Make no covenant with the people of the land." The Canaanites nations were a very sinful, degraded people. They had sinned away their hour of grace. *"The iniquity of the Amorites was now full." (Genesis 15:16)*

Israel was to be the hand of God's judgment on those wicked nations. They were to be exterminated.

When Jericho fell, all the inhabitants, except Rehab and her household who were in faith covenant with Israel, were put to the sword. After a brief setback, the city of Ai was annihilated. The next city on the hit list was the powerful city of Gibeon.

So the Gibeonites acted with cunning. They put on ragged, worn-out clothing, worn-out shoes and took bags of moldy bread and made their way to the camp of Joshua at Gilgal.

"Cut a blood covenant with us," they demanded.

Joshua and the leaders of Israel responded, "We have a mandate from our God to cut no blood covenant with the inhabitants of this land."

"But we are not of this land," they replied. "We have come from a distant country. When we left our land these were new clothes. But the long journey has caused them to wear thread-bare. This bread was hot and fresh when we left but now it's all dry and moldy. You can cut a blood covenant with us since we are from a distant land."

It was a lie. Gibeon was 26 miles from Joshua's camp at Gilgal.

But Joshua and the elders did not pray and ask guidance from God. Thus they entered into a sacred, binding covenant with a people under the sentence of death. Three days later it was discovered that they had been deceived. The people demanded that the liars be put to death. But Joshua had a deep understanding of blood covenant. He knew it was sacred. It was not to be violated.

The Gibeonites were called in and told that they would not be put to death but would be servants of the house of Israel forever.

Many years later King Saul, in the early, zealous years of his reign, attacked Gibeon and killed some Gibeonites. He had violated a sacred blood covenant. Now years later, famine is on the land because of the blood guilt that Saul had caused.

David asked the Gibeonites what he could do to make it right. The Gibeonites demanded blood. Seven of Saul's relatives were to be handed over to the Gibeonites and put to death.

"When I heard about their demand, fear struck my heart. I fit that category of people that they demanded. Would David give me over to them? Things were very tense for a few days. But the covenant between David and Dad prevailed. David spared me again. What a powerful blood covenant!" thought Mephibosheth.

WHAT DOES THIS MEAN TO ME?

Our enemy, the devil, seeks our destruction like the Gibeonites. He is always demanding that we be punished. But our God will not give us over to his demands. His love is steadfast. *"It is because of the Lord's mercies (enduring covenant love) that we are not cut off. His mercies never come to an end. They are new every morning. Great is His faithfulness." Lamentations 3:22*

The greatest Hebrew word in the Old Testament is *checed*. It is a covenant word, translated hundreds of times in the King James Bible with the word mercy. The Revised Standard Version translates it steadfast love. It is always connected to God's faithfulness. He is a covenant-making, covenant-keeping, faithful God. *"Satisfy us in the morning with your steadfast love (Heb. checed-covenant mercy) that we may rejoice and be glad all our days." Psalms 90:14 (RSV)*

Satan may rage and demand that we be turned over to him but God says, "No, way. These are my covenant kids. *I give them eternal life, and they shall never perish, and no one shall snatch them out of my hand." John 10:28 (RSV)*

"Who shall separate us from the love of Christ? Shall tribulation, or distress, or persecution, or famine, or nakedness, or peril, or sword. No, in all these things we are more than conquerors through him who loved us. For I am persuaded that neither death, nor life, nor angels, nor principalities, nor things present, nor things to come, nor powers, nor height, nor depth, nor anything else in all creation, will be able to separate us from the love of God in Christ Jesus our Lord." Romans 8:35-38 (RSV)

Then I will punish their transgression with the rod and their iniquity with scourges; but I will not remove from him my steadfast love (checed), or be false to my faithfulness. I will not violate my covenant, or alter the word that went forth from my lips. Psalms 98:32-34 (RSV)

Conclusion

"The years have skipped by so quickly. I'm now an old man. Even Cora is showing her age. David's days are numbered; he looks old and tired. But he has given instructions concerning me and my family at his death. We are to continue to stay in the palace as long as we live. The blood covenant that he cut with Jonathan and his seed will still be viable ever after David's death. How amazing is the God of Israel, King David his servant, my deceased father, and the covenant!" rejoiced Mephibosheth.